Sharpen Your Axe
52 Speaking Tips

Al Jensen

Your Powerful
To The Point
Book

Sharpen Your Axe
52 Speaking Tips

by
Al Jensen
Speaker, Author, Coach
Next Stage Communications

Sharpen Your Axe
52 Speaking Tips

Published by **To The Point**
Next Stage Communications
A Subsidiary of Next Stage Speaking

Copyright © 2019 Al Jensen

All rights reserved. No part of this book may be reproduced or transmitted in any form or by any means, electronic or mechanical, including photocopying, recording or by any information storage an retrieval system, without written permission of the publisher, except for including of brief quotations in a review.

Next Stage Communications
3638 Tioga Way
Las Vegas, NV 89169
(702) 682-8431

ISBN: 978-1-7338602-7-7

Al Jensen

Sharpen Your Axe
52 Speaking Tips

Contents

1 Start with the end in mind 1

2 Determine your takeaways 1

3 Have a clear topic/purpose 2

4 Capture your audience's attention in the speech opening 2

5 Open your speech with a quote 3

6 Open your speech with a funny story 3

7 Create a foundational phrase 4

8 Tell a story 4

9 Begin your stories by setting the scene and introducing the characters 5

10 Move your story along with Crisis/Conflict 5

11 Describe the pursuit of a goal and ultimately, a resolution of the conflict 6

12 Give your character(s) a Victory Moment 6

13 Tell the audience what the lesson (moral of the story) is 7

14 Learn Improv 7

15 Build your speech in modules 8

16 Learn transitions (aka "bridges") 8

Al Jensen

17 Pattern interrupts 9
18 Vocal variety 9
19 Master the pause 10
20 Call to action 10
21 Time 11
22 Know your rate of speech 11
23 Quotations 12
24 Nervous ticks 13
25 Incorporate humor in your speech 14
26 Be enthusiastic! 14
27 Eye contact 15
28 Rhetorical Questions 15
29 Be original 16
30 Know your topic 16
31 Use your body 17
32 Hand gestures 17
33 Facial expressions 18
34 Own the stage 18
35 Organization 19
36 Apologies 20
37 Conclusion 20

Sharpen Your Axe
52 Speaking Tips

5 Open your speech with a quote

Deliver a quote. Some philosophical thought that embodies and supports the concept and points you'll make in your address. Make sure to offer attribution to the person who offered up the saying initially.

6 Open your speech with a funny story

People love to laugh. Get off on the right foot by sharing a humorous story or anecdote. The humor should set the stage for the tone of the balance of your speech. When you condition the audience to expect funny quips early in your remarks, you'll have the audience in the palm of your hand, awaiting the next punch line. Don't underestimate the power of opening your talk with humor.

Al Jensen

7 Create a foundational phrase

A foundational phrase is ten words or less that encapsulates your topic. For example, "Don't get ready! Stay Ready!" (Thanks, Craig Valentine!) Distill your message into ten words or less. Try to find an alliteration to make it more memorable.

8 Tell a story

Stories compel audiences to listen to you. Learn the fundamental elements of storytelling and use it to draw the audience in and illustrate the point you want to convey to listeners. Keep your stories around 250-500 words and point out the lesson the story teaches.

**Sharpen Your Axe
52 Speaking Tips**

9 Begin your stories by setting the scene and introducing the characters

Define the "Before" picture of the character's everyday life. Paint the picture of life for the character while creating sympathy, empathy, jeopardy, likeability, a unique characteristic or particular skill possessed by the character

10 Move your story along with Crisis/Conflict

Define and describe the event that caused the character to realize that he/she had a serious problem that demanded to be solved. Identify and describe the character's goals and desired finish line. Include details of the characters uncertainty, doubt and possible false starts in the process of determining a course of action. Make sure to emphasize the characters emotions as a result of the crisis/conflict.

11 Describe the pursuit of a goal and ultimately, a resolution of the conflict

Describe the action steps the character took to reach the finish line. Include at least two actions. If you are guiding the character to resolution, include the ways you helped them come to the resolution. Be sure to describe the characters emotions which have changed as a result of the transformation/resolution of the crisis/conflict.

12 Give your character(s) a Victory Moment

Describe the specific moment the character crosses the finish line and realizes they've overcome the struggle. Include  details of how the life of the character has changed, including the emotional transformation as a result of overcoming the conflict. Here is where you emphasize the effects of the journey - How the character is reaping the rewards for completing the mission.

13 Tell the audience what the lesson (moral of the story) is

Here is where you put the lesson or moral, of the story into perspective for your audience. Help the listener "connect the dots" and understand how your characters struggle, resolution and victory offers a relatable lesson in their lives.

14 Learn Improv

Find an improvisational players group and join up. Go to rehearsals. Attend the workshops. Get involved in improv. Not only is it fun on its own merits, but it's also great skills training for a speaker. Trust me on this. It'll make you better in front of an audience.

15 Build your speech in modules

Our attention spans are conditioned to be limited to 7 or 8 minute time frames. When building your speech, create modules of around 600-900 words (which equates to 5 to 8 minutes). Creating a longer speech? Link 2, 3, 4 or more modules together and offer additional stories and points around your central theme.

16 Learn transitions (aka "bridges")

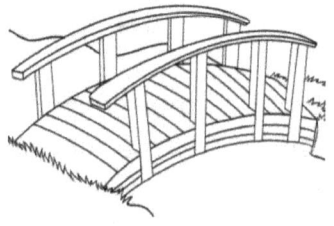

As you move from one story/point to another in your speech, a transition is what bridges the talk from one point to another. Ask yourself, "what concept ties the two talking points together"? Move seamlessly from one point to another by tying them together with a common thread.

Sharpen Your Axe
52 Speaking Tips

17 Pattern interrupts

Have you ever noticed how some speakers have a specific, noticeable rhythm or cadence to their speech? Ever get lulled to sleep by that cadence? Chances are you have a cadence in your speech patterns as well. Break up your cadence/pattern with an "interrupt" every 4-6 minutes. It could be an alliteration or phrase that is inconsistent with your message, a funny voice, a short quip or joke.....anything to break up the rhythmic cadence to your presentation.

18 Vocal variety

Vocal variety can serve as a pattern interrupt and keep your audience engaged. Vocal variety means variety in power (volume), pitch and pace. Learn how to show emotions with your voice. Use slow, low tones to convey sadness or higher pitch and a quicker pace to express excitement. The vocal variety emphasizes the words you use you apply.

19 Master the pause

Pauses signal the movement from one point to another and are frequently used to allow the audience to ponder a question posed by the speaker. Pauses are also a pattern interrupt. Use different length pauses throughout your speech for dramatic effect and to allow listeners to answer a rhetorical question in their mind, or contemplate the points you're making.

20 Call to action

Ideas without action are worthless. If you want listeners to adopt your point of view, achieve a goal or take a specific action, you need to be specific in your call to action. In the conclusion of your speech, while tying all of your points together, be specific in the action steps you want the listeners to take.

**Sharpen Your Axe
52 Speaking Tips**

21 Time

Most every time you speak, you will have a particular time period to fill. Event organizers want you to fill that time without going short or going long. Know the time limits and develop a system for watching your time. That little time keeping device in the back corners of your mind goes haywire when you're speaking in front of an audience. Set up your smartphone, tablet or another device to count up or count down the minutes and seconds you have to complete your remarks

22 Know your rate of speech

To stay within the time guidelines of your remarks, knowing your typical rate of speech is an important detail to know as you write your speech. How do you calculate your rate of speech? Record yourself giving various speeches and then

transcribe those speeches, noting every word spoken. Divide the total number of words spoken by the minutes it took you to deliver the speech, and you'll have your personal, unique rate of speech. Rates will differ based on the type of speech you give and the emotions you relate, so do this calculation over several speeches to learn your numbers and variables.

23 Quotations

Quotes are an excellent method of making a point or building emotional connections with your audience. They are particularly handy when you're trying to present a topic or concept that is uncommonly difficult for an audience to grasp.

Sharpen Your Axe
52 Speaking Tips

24 Nervous ticks

Do you pull at your earlobe? Clasp your hands in front of you? Scratch your head? Tap your fingers on the lectern? Ask a friend to watch for any apparent nervous ticks when you speak. Reviewing the video of your speech may help you see what they are talking about. Self-review is better than nothing but try to get someone else to provide feedback on what nervous ticks you exhibit which may be distracting from your message. Next time you speak, make it a point to avoid those nervous ticks and develop better speaking habits.

25 Incorporate humor in your speech

Not every speech should be funny, but humor can be used as pattern interrupts and a tool to make dry subjects more appealing to listeners. Stick to clean humor to not offend anyone in the audience. Read a book, take a class or find a joke you can twist to make it uniquely your own. Jokes found on the internet or in joke books are typically not a good idea unless you re-write it to make it unique to your story.

26 Be enthusiastic!

Be in the moment, with energy and enthusiasm when you speak to an audience. A successful speech ultimately transfers your passion for a topic to the listener. Bring your enthusiasm and your audience's attention will never waiver.

Sharpen Your Axe
52 Speaking Tips

27 Eye contact

An old proverb suggests that the eyes are the mirror of the soul. Speakers who don't make good eye contact are often thought of as being embarrassed, weak or hiding something. Make eye contact to engage your listeners and help them know you are sincere in your efforts to convey your message to them. Try to keep eye contact with one audience member (or section of the audience in large venues) per point. One person - one point.

28 Rhetorical Questions

A rhetorical question is one which is not expected to be answered aloud. It can be used to introduce explanations: "So, why then is it important to understand the history of war?" It can be used to allow the audience members to associate

their own experiences to your topic: "Have you ever had a dreadful day at work?"

29 Be original

Humans prefer the unique, novelty. What makes your speech unique or original? Did you introduce a new fact? Did you present an original interpretation of a widely known fact or theory? Did you suggest insight into something commonly known? Don't deliver dry facts. Make it interesting by sharing your unique point of view.

30 Know your topic

When asked what they speak on, many speakers respond "I can speak on anything." Don't be like those speakers. Know your topic. Be an expert on the subject. Don't speak on an issue just because you can. Speak about something because you are called to deliver a unique perspective or message to a hungry audience.

**Sharpen Your Axe
52 Speaking Tips**

31 Use your body

Words are but one of the ways in which we communicate our message to an audience. The posture we take, the facial expressions we make, the way we move around the stage with purpose...all contribute to the message we deliver to our listeners. Most effective speakers don't hide behind the lectern; they get out front, up close and personal to their audiences. Move about, but CAUTION: Move with purpose. Movement for the sake of moving is distracting.

32 Hand gestures

 Generally, hands should be kept out of your pockets (distracting), your arms should not be crossed (appears defensive), and generally, should not be hidden. Keep your hands by your side until you desire to use them to emphasize a point or focus the audience's attention. Good uses of hand gestures include counting items on your fingers, pointing at locations, demonstrating relative size of objects, or miming the existence of imaginary obstacles.

33 Facial expressions

When we listen to others, we typically look at the speakers face. Facial expressions are an essential part of the communications process. Learn to match your facial expressions to the emotions you're expressing in your speech. Exaggerating your facial expressions is a great way to emphasize humor, sadness, fear or other emotions you want the audience to receive. Think congruity in your facial expressions.

34 Own the stage

Are you shaking when delivering your speech? Quivering voice? Breaking out in a sweat? Uncomfortable? Confidence is contagious. If you're confident, your audience is confident. If you're nervous, your audience is too. The best way to increase trust is to speak to one person at a

Sharpen Your Axe
52 Speaking Tips

time in the audience, and practice and prepare your message. There's no substitution for practicing in a safe environment. Perfect practice makes perfect performances.

35 Organization

A good speech is more than a random assortment and delivery of facts. It must be ordered so the audience can

- First item.
- Second item.
- Third item.

understand it. Order it chronological (earliest to latest), topical (point by point), problem/solution (discuss a problem then a means to solve it), or spatial (discuss different locations, one at a time). Grab the audience's attention, tell them what you're going to tell them, tell them, then tell them what you told them and ask them to take specific action as a result of your speech.

36 Apologies

As a rule, don't apologize. Apologies break the flow of your message and might even call your professionalism or ability to speak on the topic into question.

You're giving the gift of your knowledge and insights to the audience, and there is rarely a need to apologize from the platform.

37 Conclusion

If you're a great speechwriter, you started writing your speech with your end in mind. You already know what points and takeaways you want the audience to remember. Take a second look at the conclusion and see if you can trim any unnecessary words. This is the place to be as succinct as possible. Don't be abrupt, but make sure to summarize your points and deliver a clear call to action.

Sharpen Your Axe
52 Speaking Tips

38 Visuals and props

"A picture is worth a thousand words." ~ Old proverb Not every speech requires props or visuals, but they can add to a speech. Just remember,  visuals or props are there to support your message, not to take its place. As a general rule if you use slides, use large, easy to read text with as few words as possible (generally less than 12 words per slide). Never read the slides or turn your back to the audience. Avoid "passing around" a prop as it almost always causes a distraction from your message.

39 Be succinct

"The most valuable of all talents is that of never using two words when one will do" ~ Thomas Jefferson. Each word should add to your speech. Don't use additional words to "fill time" in your speech. Great speeches aren't written, they're re-written. After writing your address, look for words that can be pruned from the text. Make every word count.

40 Vocal volume

Speak so audience members in the rear of the room can hear you clearly, while at the same time making sure those in the front don't think you're yelling at them. Get to the speaking venue before the audience so you can get a feel for what kind of volume is required. Ask someone to stand at the back of the room as you speak so you can get a feel for the volume needed. Increasing volume can show emphasis while reducing volume can draw the audience in with anticipation of what you'll say next. Use a variety of volumes in your speech to create a compelling "texture" of your message.

41 Know your audience

Match the content of your message with the receptivity of your audience. If you speak about the benefits of

Sharpen Your Axe
52 Speaking Tips

long term care insurance, you're not going to be well received at a children's library lecture series. Also, it's essential to match the knowledge level of the audience with your message. Example: If you speak on the intricacies of quantum physics, you might not connect with a Junior High school science class.

42 Introductions

Write your introduction for the MC to deliver. A good introduction will set the stage for your speech, establish you as an authority and worthiness of speaking to the audience. Write your introduction in the third person, keeping it short and sweet, typically around 50-75 words for a speech of 10 minutes or less and up to 125 words for addresses up to 60 minutes in length.

43 Wardrobe

Dress to validate the level of professionalism and/or credibility you want to convey to the audience. Practicing a speech in front of friends is one thing, but when speaking to an audience who is anxiously looking forward to hearing your content is another. Be professional and keep away from the provocative. It's a speech, not a fashion show. If possible, take into consideration the color of the background you'll be speaking in front of. Solid or simple patterns in muted tones are generally called for.

44 Smile!

While your facial expressions should be congruent with the tone and emotion you intend to convey. During those times you're not expressing an emotion, SMILE! Let your audience know you're pleased to be able to share your message with them. Smiles are contagious. Your audience will be at ease and anxious to hear your message when you share your smile with them!

45 Videotape your speeches

Sharpen Your Axe
52 Speaking Tips

Every time you speak to an audience, be it rehearsal, practice or a full-fledged delivery -VIDEOTAPE YOURSELF! You may argue you don't like to watch yourself on tape or you don't like your voice. GET OVER IT! The audience had to watch and listen to you, what makes you so unique you don't need to watch yourself? Video review is the best method for improving your performance. Don't like your posture? Work on changing it. Didn't smile enough? You'll notice when you watch the tape!

46 Find someone to evaluate your speech

Ask someone you admire and respect to review your video and provide feedback. Do not seek input from others who are at your level of expertise, but from someone who performs at a higher level than you do. Ask them for their honest opinion so you can focus on improving the areas that need it. Also, ask them what they liked about your presentation so you can make sure to repeat it next time.

Al Jensen

47 Speak often

World Champion of Public Speaking Darren LaCroix's mantra is Stage Time, Stage Time, Stage Time. He suggests you never pass up the opportunity to speak in front of an audience. I concur. Once I committed to speak 100 times in 6 months. That was the most amazing growth period in my speaking career. I videotaped and reviewed each performance. If you want to advance your speaking skills by quantum leaps, speak often.

48 Learn from your mistakes

When you review a speech you've delivered, pay particular attention to those issues that need your attention. Don't cut yourself down for making mistakes. Instead, congratulate yourself for taking the time to identify a poor habit that needs attention. No one gets better by continuing to rehearse the same mistakes over and over. No one delivers a perfect speech the

Sharpen Your Axe
52 Speaking Tips

first time out. Learn from your mistakes and the next speech will be better and the next time you write a new speech, the learning/improvement curve will be much shorter.

49 Repeat your successes

Each time you speak, upon review of your performance, you'll notice some aspects of your delivery that came off exceptionally well. Maybe by design, perhaps by accident. Regardless of the cause, make a note of what went exceptionally well and make a point to repeat it next time you speak in front of an audience.

50 Create a media kit

One truth in speaking is "Speaking begets speaking." This means that the more you speak, the more opportunities you'll get to speak. Speak at a group on Tuesday, and someone will come up to you and ask if you're available a week from Saturday. Be prepared with a demo video of your speeches, a one-sheet highlighting your topics and biography. Get a good quality headshot and an action shot of you speaking. Prospective speaker bookers want to see you, hear you and understand your qualifications to talk to their group. Be prepared when opportunity knocks.

51 Join Toastmasters, Speakers Clubs, National Speakers Association

The speaking world is filled with  amazing organizations dedicated to helping you become a better and more engaging speaker. Reach out and take part in those organizations which cater to up and coming speakers just like you. You'll continue to expand your comfort zone and make some powerful relationships which will serve you well in your journey.

Sharpen Your Axe
52 Speaking Tips

52 Hire a speaking coach

If you're serious about taking your speaking skills to the next level, sooner rather than later, shorten your learning curve by engaging a speaker coach who will help you "up your game" in the shortest amount of time possible. A coach can help identify your strengths and weaknesses and develop a custom plan of exercises and approaches to help you shorten your learning curve.

The tips in this booklet are designed to stimulate your thinking. Help you find areas of your speaking endeavors that might benefit from a little attention. In many cases, personal reflection might be adequate. In other instances, significant study, rehearsal, and improvements might be called for. Work on it yourself, discuss the concepts and ideas with a friend, or consider hiring a speech coach to help you develop more thoroughly and quickly as a speaker. There's no substitute for professional assistance.

Al Jensen

If you've enjoyed these speaking tips and would like more details, please drop me an e-mail to Al@AlJensen.com. I'm continually developing additional training materials, including books, videos, online training courses as well as in-person and virtual coaching programs.

Cheers! Here's to being a more prosperous and effective communicator from the stage!

Sharpen Your Axe
52 Speaking Tips

About the Author

Good speakers aren't born. They're made. Al Jensen has been helping speakers, of all skill levels, write, rewrite and deliver audience engaging messages, aka: "Sharpening Their Speaking Skills" for more than ten years.

Believing that anyone can learn to be a great speaker, Al is a master at helping his clients find their core message and deliver it professionally and engagingly.

His speaking and entertainment career began as a teenager and has grown to include adult education instruction, association and industry presentations, keynote speeches, radio talk show hosting, internet TV personality, and even a comedy magic stage act!

Based in Las Vegas, Al works with emerging as well as seasoned speakers all over the world who want to make a more dynamic impact on their audiences.

Al Jensen

This tips booklet provides an overview of the 52+ components of a speech that Al considers when coaching a speaker of any skill level. You can use the tips as a self-evaluation tool, a sort of "starting spot" for your speech growth or to help you identify areas of speaking where you might want some professional assistance.

Al provides a variety of training programs, ranging from booklets to books, online training programs, group coaching sessions, speech clubs, speaker mastermind groups, one-on-one live coaching and one-on-one virtual coaching for speakers anywhere in the English-speaking world!

Reach out and contact Al:

Al Jensen: Speaker - Author - Coach

702-883-1980 (voice or text)

AlJensen.com

Al@AlJensen.com

Want to Improve your speaking contact:

info@nextstagecommunications.com

www.ingramcontent.com/pod-product-compliance
Lightning Source LLC
Chambersburg PA
CBHW070943160426
43193CB00011B/1787